FORENS

The Doctor of Death

Harold Shipman – The World's Worst Serial Killer

by Mikaela Sitford

Manchester
EveningNews

SHIPMAN TO SPEND REST OF LIFE IN JAIL

GUILTY!

Copyright © ticktock Entertainment Ltd 2007

First published in Great Britain in 2007 by ticktock Media Ltd,
2 Orchard Business Centre, North Farm Road, Tunbridge Wells, Kent, TN2 3XF

ticktock project editor: Joe Harris
ticktock project designer: Hayley Terry
Series consultant: Dr John P Cassella

ISBN: 978 1 84696 513 5 pbk

Printed in China

Picture credits (t=top; b=bottom; c=centre; l=left; r=right; OBC=outside back cover;
OFC=outside front cover): Arresting Images (Mikael Karlsson): 30. Cavendish Press: 6t, 9, 10,
12, 15bl, 16t, 16b, 18b, 21tl, 22, 23b, 25br, 25tl, 26b. Flatearthimages.com: 17b. Michael D
Hunter M.D: 29. iStockphoto: OBCb, (Timothy Large) 19. Manchester Evening News/ MEN
Syndication: OBCt, 1, 4b, 5t, 6b, 13, 18t, 24t, 26t, 27t, 27c. Phil Noble/PA Archive/PA Photos:
20. PA/PA Archive/PA Photos: 24b, 25tl. Rex Features: 28. Science Photo Library: 7b
(MAURO FERMARIELLO), 11bl (Colin Cuthbert), 14 (DR JURGEN SCRIBA). Shutterstock:
OFC, 2, 3, 5tr, 5b, 7tr, 7t, 8, 9tr, 11tr, 11br, 13tr, 15tr, 15br, 17tr, 19tr, 21tr, 21b, 23tr, 23t, 25tr.
ticktock Media Archive: 4t, 17c.

Contents

A Suspicious Will

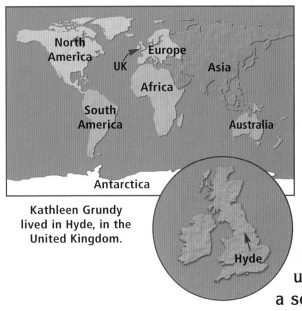

Kathleen Grundy lived in Hyde, in the United Kingdom.

On 24th June 1998, two friends found Kathleen Grundy dead at her home in Hyde, near Manchester. They were worried when she did not appear at a lunch club she helped run. They went to her house to check that she was okay. They found the door unlocked. She was lying on a sofa and looked asleep.

Kathleen Grundy's concerned friends called her doctor, Harold Shipman. He pronounced her dead and said the cause of death was 'old age'. The police were also called, but they did not suspect the death was unnatural.

Kathleen Grundy's home, Loughrigg Cottage.

TRUE LIFE
CRIME
TRUE LIFE

FORENSIC FACTFILE

A Mysterious Death

Kathleen Grundy

The victim:
Kathleen Grundy, an 81-year-old widow who lived alone. She had once been the Mayor of Hyde.

Date of death:
24th June 1998

Crime scene:
The lounge at her home, Loughrigg Cottage

Health:
Kathleen Grundy was very fit for her age. She worked in local charity shops. She also ran a lunch club for pensioners.

On the same day as Kathleen Grundy died, a suspicious **will** arrived at a **solicitor**'s office. Was it really Kathleen Grundy's will, or had it been **forged**?

The suspicious will was the first clue in a major investigation.

Kathleen Grundy, a wealthy widow, had trusted Dr Shipman. In fact, she seemed to have left all she owned to Dr Shipman in her will. He was the last person to see her alive. An investigation into her will was to end 23 years of murder by Britain's worst **serial killer**.

Angela Woodruff Investigates

Kathleen Grundy's daughter, Angela Woodruff, read her mother's **will**. It was badly written and looked scruffy, unlike her mother's other paperwork, which was neat and well-organised. Also, it was odd that she had left nothing to her family, who she loved.

Angela Woodruff began to think that the will had been forged. She wondered if someone was trying to **frame** Dr Shipman, and make it look like he had killed her mother. Soon, though, she began to suspect something much worse...

Angela Woodruff was determined to find out how her mother really died.

> *Angela Woodruff began to think the will had been forged.*

Harold Shipman had worked as a GP in Hyde since 1977. He opened his own clinic on Market Street, Hyde, in 1993.

Angela Woodruff spoke to the two **witnesses** named on the will. They said that Dr Shipman had asked them to sign something, but it was not a will.

The signatures on the will were **forgeries**. Angela Woodruff thought that Dr Shipman had tricked the witnesses into signing another document, and then copied their signatures. He had done this so he could inherit Kathleen Grundy's money.

Forging a signature on a will is a crime.

FORENSIC FACTFILE
The Fingerprint Evidence

- The police examined the will for fingerprints. There were none belonging to Kathleen Grundy. However they did find something at the bottom of one page. It was a print from Dr Shipman's little finger. Why would Dr Shipman's fingerprint be on the will of his patient?

- Whenever anyone touches a surface, their fingers leave a mark called a fingerprint. The fingerprint left by each finger of every human being is unique.

A police detective looks at a fingerprint enlarged on a computer screen.

How Kathleen Grundy Died

Kathleen Grundy's diary was helpful to the police.

Angela Woodruff wanted to find out the truth about her mother's sudden death. She spoke to Kathleen Grundy's friends and read her diary.

Kathleen Grundy's friends said she had been very well in the days before she died. She had told her best friend, May Clarke, that Dr Shipman was coming to take a blood **sample**. He had said this was for a survey about ageing by the University of Manchester.

Kathleen Grundy had also written about taking part in the survey in her diary. She wrote that Dr Shipman had asked her to take part because she was very fit and well for her age. If this was the case, why had she died suddenly of old age, as Dr Shipman claimed?

Dr Shipman said he wanted to take a blood sample. Was this true?

Dr Shipman became the prime suspect in a criminal investigation.

Angela Woodruff now suspected that Dr Shipman had murdered her mother. She told the Greater Manchester Police what she had found, and an investigation was opened.

FORENSIC FACTFILE
The Fake Survey

- Dr Shipman had said he needed a blood sample as part of a survey for the University of Manchester.

- The police contacted the University of Manchester. They said that they were not carrying out a survey on ageing at that time.

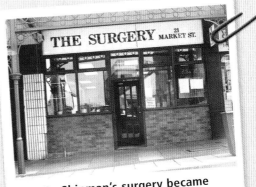

Dr Shipman's surgery became a potential crime scene.

- After taking a blood sample, a doctor will send the sample on to a **pathology laboratory**. When the police contacted the pathology laboratory, they said they had not received any sample for Kathleen Grundy.

Linda Reynolds' Warning

The death of Kathleen Grundy was not the first time people were suspicious about Dr Shipman. In March 1998, fellow doctor, Linda Reynolds had noticed that many of Dr Shipman's patients were dying.

In fact, Dr Shipman's patients' **death rate** was five times higher than other doctors'. Linda Reynolds was worried about this. She reported this fact to the coroner.

Dr Shipman (circled) with his colleagues at Market Street Surgery, Hyde, in 1995.

Detective Inspector Dave Smith led the first investigation.

The police decided to investigate. Detective Inspector Dave Smith, a detective with the Greater Manchester Police, worked on the case for nearly a month. However in the end, Smith couldn't prove anything against Dr Shipman. He told Linda Reynolds that Shipman was innocent.

FORENSIC FACTFILE

The First Investigation

- Dave Smith interviewed Linda Reynolds about Dr Shipman's death rate.
- Dave Smith looked at the **death certificates** for 19 of Dr Shipman's patients who had died in the previous six months. Everything looked normal.

Missed Chances

- Dave Smith did not carry out a forensic investigation, although it would have been quite easy to do so. At the time there were two bodies of Dr Shipman's patients at a local funeral parlour. They could have been given **toxicology** tests. These tests would have shown if the patients had been poisoned.
- The police did not check Dr Shipman's criminal record. He had broken the law by using his position as a doctor to steal painkilling drugs. He had been **addicted** to them.

A toxicology test is carried out on a sample of muscle tissue.

Dr Shipman had stolen painkillers from his surgery.

The First Exhumation

When the suspicious death of Kathleen Grundy was linked to Dr Shipman, the Greater Manchester Police carried out another investigation. They interviewed Kathleen Grundy's friends, and spoke to the **witnesses** named on her will.

The police needed to examine Kathleen Grundy's body to find out whether she had been murdered. This led to the first **exhumation** in the history of the Greater Manchester Police.

First they asked permission from Kathleen Grundy's family. Then on 1st August 1998 they removed her body from its grave. The date was exactly one month after she was buried.

After the exhumation, the coffin was taken to a **mortuary**. The body was still inside it.

Kathleen Grundy's body was buried in the cemetery of Hyde Chapel.

TRUE LIFE
CRIME
TRUE LIFE

The police carried out the exhumation during the night, so that people would not find out about it.

FORENSIC FACTFILE

Exhumation

Exhumation is the removal of a body from its grave. It is very unusual for police to do this.

It is also illegal to exhume a body without following certain steps.
You need:

• Permission from the government (in the UK this is the Home Office).

• Permission from religious leaders, if the person is buried in a cemetery belonging to a church, mosque or temple.

A tent was set up over Kathleen Grundy's grave while police performed the exhumation.

The Post-Mortem

Dr John Rutherford carried out a post mortem on Kathleen Grundy's body. It showed that she was fit and healthy. That meant there was no natural cause for her death.

Dr Rutherford sent small samples of Kathleen Grundy's muscle and liver to a lab for toxicology tests. These tests can show when someone has been poisoned. The samples contained a large amount of a drug called **morphine**. The tests proved that Kathleen Grundy had been killed by an injection of morphine.

Dr Rutherford also had Kathleen Grundy's hair tested. Each time someone takes morphine, small amounts stay in their hair. The tests showed that Kathleen Grundy had not taken morphine before. This fact became very important later.

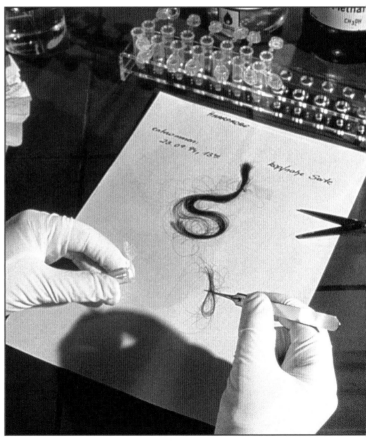

Experts examined Kathleen Grundy's hair for traces of morphine.

As a doctor, Harold Shipman would easily be able to get hold of morphine. When the police searched his home, they found that he had stored large amounts of double-strength morphine, or diamorphine. The police now suspected that Dr Shipman injected Kathleen Grundy with this drug when he visited her to take a blood test.

FORENSIC FACTFILE
Morphine and Diamorphine

- Morphine is a **painkiller** used in hospitals. It is related to the illegal drug heroin.

- Diamorphine is the same drug as morphine, but twice as strong. Dr Shipman had stored large amounts of it. He did this by requesting too much for patients, and keeping the extra doses.

- Police were surprised that Dr Shipman used morphine to poison patients. A doctor should have known that drugs of this type can stay in bodies for years. They have even been found in Egyptian mummies – which are thousands of years old!

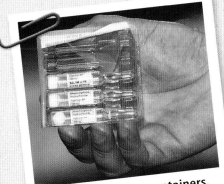

Morphine in glass containers.

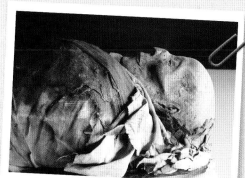

Drugs like morphine have been found in Egyptian mummies.

TRUE LIFE CRIME TRUE LIFE

The police searched Dr Shipman's home and office in August 1998. They found the typewriter used for the forged will.

Dr Shipman claimed Kathleen Grundy had borrowed it. However when the police dusted the keys for fingerprints, they did not find any belonging to Kathleen Grundy.

Police officers took **medical records** from Dr Shipman's surgery. They also made a copy of the office computer's **hard disk**. This contained records of patients' visits, Dr Shipman's notes, and the treatment given.

The typewriter used to type Kathleen Grundy's will.

TRUE LIFE CRIME TRUE LIFE

Security guards outside Dr Shipman's surgery, on Market Street in Hyde.

However, Kathleen Grundy's medical records included information that was later shown to be false. They suggested that she had been a heroin addict.

Dr Shipman had also recorded fake appointments in the medical records. But these did not agree with Kathleen Grundy's diary. One appointment supposedly took place when she was actually staying with her daughter.

FORENSIC FACTFILE
Credit Card Records

The police could tell that Dr Shipman had faked some of Kathleen Grundy's appointments by looking at his credit card records.

Each credit card has a unique code which can be traced by the police. Dr Shipman's card would have looked something like this.

- Each time someone uses their credit card, a message is sent to the credit card company. The company makes a record of the date and time, and the person's location.

- The police can approach a credit card company and ask to see their records.

- Dr Shipman had made a note of an appointment with Kathleen Grundy in Hyde. However his credit card records showed that at the time he had actually been on a shopping trip to York.

The police studied Dr Shipman's credit card records.

The Exhumations Continue

A tent was placed over each grave to shield it from view.

The police began to suspect that Kathleen Grundy was not Dr Shipman's only victim. To find out if he had murdered other patients, they needed to carry out more exhumations.

The bodies of 11 more of Dr Shipman's patients were removed from their graves over the next four months. Some of the bodies had been buried as long as six years. All of the bodies were given toxicology tests.

The tests showed that eight of these patients had died from morphine overdoses. However they were not morphine addicts, and their medical records showed that they had never been **prescribed** morphine.

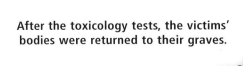

After the toxicology tests, the victims' bodies were returned to their graves.

IN
LOVING MEMORY
OF
KATHLEEN GRUNDY
2·7·1916 - 24·6·1998
WIFE OF JOHN
MOTHER OF ANGELA
GRANDMOTHER OF
RICHARD AND MATTHEW
DIED UNEXPECTEDLY AFTER A
LIFETIME OF HELPING OTHERS

The police now knew that they were dealing with a serial killer, who had killed many people by poisoning them with drugs. Harold Shipman had tried to hide his guilt by having his victims **cremated**. He had requested Kathleen Grundy's cremation in the fake will. If her body had been cremated, it would have been much harder to find out how she died.

FORENSIC FACTFILE

Other Evidence

- Relatives told the police that all the victims were found sitting or lying with their clothes neat and tidy. If the victims had suffered strokes or heart attacks, as Shipman claimed, they would have struggled.

- Dr Shipman's records showed that he was the last person to see his victims. Relatives said that he was sometimes present when his patients died.

- Evidence such as Kathleen Grundy's diary showed that Dr Shipman had lied about why he had visited the victims. He had not been invited to visit them because they felt ill.

- The records of the Greater Manchester Ambulance Service showed that Dr Shipman did not call for ambulances from the scene.

Dr Shipman failed to call an ambulance, although he was with his patients as they died.

The Computer

The computer's hard disk was the key to Harold Shipman's downfall. There were errors in the paper records, but he could excuse these as innocent mistakes. For example, he claimed that he made a mistake recording an appointment with Kathleen Grundy for the day he was in York. He said that while filling in the medical notes, he had simply put the wrong date down.

But the computer's hard disk showed the true, terrible pattern. Dr Shipman had changed the records for each victim within hours of having murdered them. His aim was to make it look like they were very ill, and they died because of their illness.

Dr Shipman's office. Police found important evidence on his computer.

Maureen Ward was killed by Dr Shipman on 18th February, 1998. He claimed she died of a brain tumour.

In the case of one patient, Maureen Ward, the computer notes said that she died of a brain tumour. Dr Shipman had also noted this 'fact' on her **death certificate**. He had changed her notes to mention a brain tumour only 45 minutes before he killed her!

FORENSIC FACTFILE
Evidence on Computers

- When someone saves data on a computer, they leave a record called a 'shadow' on the computer's hard disk. This shows when an entry is made, even if the user tries to add a false date. It is impossible to fake this information.

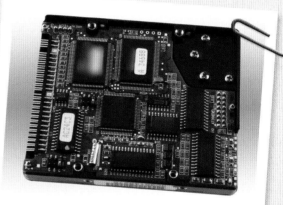

A computer's hard disk.

- The police gave the hard disk of Dr Shipman's computer to a computer examination team. This team was able to see exactly when Dr Shipman made entries about patients.

- Police could prove that it was Dr Shipman who changed the records. Only he had a password. He had also admitted earlier that he personally had made the entries.

The Police Interviews

Police first interviewed Harold Shipman on 14th August 1998. At the time, the powerful evidence on the computer was not yet known. Shipman thought he could explain all the evidence against him. He used special medical terms to try to confuse police.

At the second interview, on 7th September 1998, officers asked about the computer. Dr Shipman admitted he himself entered the appointment records. He also agreed that he had made notes saying that patients were seriously ill.

" Dr Shipman, knowing he had been found out, fell to his knees. "

Dr Shipman after his arrest, with two police officers.

The police officers then told Dr Shipman how the hard disk had recorded the entries' real dates. They showed him all the fake entries made near the time of the deaths.

Dr Shipman, knowing he had been found out, fell to his knees. He was sobbing. On 7th September, the police charged him with killing Kathleen Grundy.

The computer evidence was the key to proving Shipman's guilt.

FORENSIC FACTFILE

How the Police Trapped Shipman

- The police knew that Dr Shipman was not a computer expert. Detectives used this to trick Shipman into an important confession.

- In interviews, the detectives made Shipman feel relaxed and confident. They asked him simple questions about computers. The questions led Shipman to admit that only he could have made the computer entries.

The police used Shipman's ignorance to trap him.

- Dr Shipman thought he understood computers well. He did not realise that the hard disk showed exactly when he had made each entry.

Guilty!

Manchester
EveningNews

SHIPMAN TO SPEND REST OF LIFE IN JAIL

GUILTY!

After Dr Shipman was charged with Kathleen Grundy's murder he was **remanded** in prison. Between September 1998 and February 1999 he was charged with another 14 murders.

Nine of his patients' bodies had been exhumed, and showed signs of morphine poisoning. The other six patients had been cremated.

The trial of Harold Shipman began on 5th October 1999, and lasted four months. On 31st January 2000, the jury found Dr Shipman guilty of all 15 murders. He was sentenced to life imprisonment.

A year after Dr Shipman was sent to prison, an inquiry was set up. One of the Shipman Inquiry's goals was to find out about other possible murders. In 2002, the inquiry reported that Shipman had murdered at least 215 people, and possibly as many as 260.

TRUE LIFE
CRIME
TRUE LIFE

Most of Harold Shipman's victims were women.

Dr Shipman was first imprisoned in Frankland Prison, near Durham, then moved to Wakefield Prison, in West Yorkshire. He hanged himself in his cell on 13th January 2004. He had never admitted his guilt.

Wakefield Prison

FORENSIC FACTFILE
The Shipman Inquiry

- The Shipman Inquiry began work in February 2001. It was led by Dame Janet Smith.

- Between 2001 and 2005 the inquiry took about 2,500 statements from witnesses. It looked at evidence from the police and health authorities.

- The inquiry's first report was published on 19th July 2002. Dame Janet Smith said that in addition to the 15 victims from the court case, Harold Shipman had killed between 200 and 245 other people.

- All of the victims had been his patients. The first was Eva Lyons in March 1975. The last was Kathleen Grundy in June 1998.

Dame Janet Smith

Case Closed

24th June 1998

Kathleen Grundy was found dead at her home in Hyde, near Manchester.

4th July 1998

Kathleen Grundy's daughter, Angela Woodruff, was told that her mother had left all she owned to Dr Harold Shipman. Thinking the will had been forged, she contacted the police.

1st August 1998

Police exhumed Kathleen Grundy's body. The post-mortem showed that she had been killed by the drug morphine.

7th August 1998

Police searched Dr Shipman's house. They found large amounts of morphine.

14th August 1998

Police searched Dr Shipman's surgery. They found the typewriter on which the will had been written.

The police found fake appointments in Dr Shipman's written records and on the hard disk of his office computer.

7th September 1998

Police interviewed Dr Shipman. He admitted that only he could have made the fake appointment records on the computer.

Dr Shipman was charged with the murder of Kathleen Grundy.

September to December 1998

The bodies of 11 more of Shipman's patients were exhumed. Eight of them had been killed by morphine – nine including Kathleen Grundy.

5th October 1999

Harold Shipman's trial began.

31st January 2000

Dr Shipman was found guilty of murdering 15 patients. He was sentenced to life in prison.

19th July 2002

The Shipman Inquiry reported that in all Harold Shipman had murdered between 215 and 260 people from 1975 to 1998.

Exhumations

Exhumations are carried out when the police need to perform a **post-mortem** on a body that has already been buried.

- Exhumations normally take place at night, so that they can be as private as possible.

- During exhumations, a white tent is set up over the grave. This hides the process from onlookers.

- Specialist lighting is used to make the scene as bright as possible.

- After the exhumation, the body is transported to a mortuary in a body bag. A post-mortem is carried out, and then the body is returned to its grave.

An environmental health officer must be present during an exhumation. Their job is to:

- Make sure that the dead person is treated with respect.

- Make sure that public health is protected. Corpses can carry diseases.

The tents used by police during exhumations protect evidence and hide it from public view.

Post-mortems

When the police need to know how someone died, they will request a post-mortem. During a post-mortem, an expert called a forensic pathologist examines the dead body to find out the cause of death. Another word for post-mortem is autopsy.

- The body is laid out on an autopsy table, cut open, and every part of it is examined for injury.

- The forensic pathologist makes a t-shaped cut across the shoulders and down to the groin to open up the body.

- Internal organs, such as the heart, stomach and lungs, are taken out. Pathologists are looking for anything unusual.

- **Samples** of the internal organs are sent to a toxicology laboratory for analysis. This is especially important if poisoning is suspected.

- After this, the organs are returned to the body.

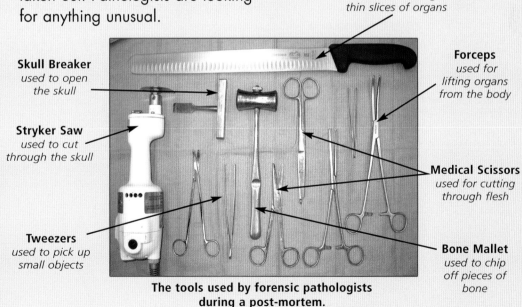

Bread Knife
used for cutting thin slices of organs

Forceps
used for lifting organs from the body

Skull Breaker
used to open the skull

Stryker Saw
used to cut through the skull

Medical Scissors
used for cutting through flesh

Tweezers
used to pick up small objects

Bone Mallet
used to chip off pieces of bone

The tools used by forensic pathologists during a post-mortem.

Toxicology

- Toxicology is the study of the harmful effects of drugs or poisons on people. It can show which chemicals have caused someone to become ill or die.

- Toxicology tests only need small amounts of hair, tissue, blood or urine. These samples are tested with various chemicals, and are examined under a microscope. A toxicology test can check for one specific drug, or as many as 30 different drugs.

- One kind of toxicology test uses hair. As hair grows, different chemicals are stored in it. A single strand of hair can act as a timeline, showing what chemicals have been in the body at different times as it has grown. Forensic scientists can measure how often a drug has been used by looking at a single strand of hair. They cut hair into small pieces, and test each piece using chemicals. This method can show whether someone was a regular drug user, or whether they were given a drug only once.

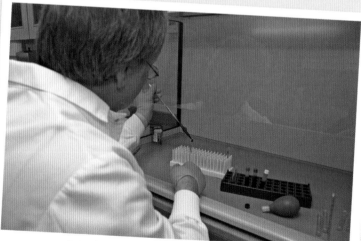

A toxicologist tests samples for traces of poison.

Glossary

addicted: To be unable to cope without something, for example a drug.

coroner: An official who investigates suspicious deaths.

cremation: Burning a corpse into ashes.

death certificate: A document, signed by a doctor, which gives the time and cause of someone's death.

death rate: The number of people dying over a set length of time.

exhumation: Removing a corpse from its grave to examine it.

forensic: Using science in the investigation of a crime.

forensic pathologist: A doctor who performs post-mortems and is trained to work out how someone died.

forged: Fake or copied, in order to trick people.

forgery: A fake document.

frame: To make it look as though someone has committed a crime, when they are innocent.

hard disk: A disk fixed inside a computer, which stores information.

inherit: To receive money or belongings from someone when they die.

medical records: Information about a patient kept by their doctor.

morphine: A painkilling drug, which must be prescribed by doctors.

mortuary: A place where dead bodies are kept before they are buried or cremated.

painkiller: A drug which reduces feelings of pain.

pathology laboratory: A place where the causes of diseases are studied.

post-mortem: The medical examination of a corpse, to find out how and when a person died.

prescribe: To advise someone to take a drug or medicine.

remand: To keep in prison until a trial.

sample: A small amount of a substance which can be used in a scientific test.

serial killer: A murderer who has killed three or more people.

solicitor: A lawyer who works for and advises people, but who does not appear in court.

toxicology: The scientific study of poisoning.

widow: A woman whose husband has died.

will: A document which says who should receive someone's money and belongings after their death.

witness: Someone who watches a document being signed, or who sees a crime being committed.

Index